WITHDRAWN

Look closely to discover a camouflaged critter hiding in this fallen foliage!

WHAT IN THE WORLD?

LOOK AGAIN

REBECCA BAINES

NATIONAL
GEOGRAPHIC

WASHINGTON, D.C.

HOW TO PLAY

YOUR BRAIN ON PUZZLES! You rely on your vision and your brain to understand the world around you. But as amazing as your eyes are, the pictures they send your brain are quirky: They're upside down, backward, and two-dimensional! Your brain automatically flips the images from your retinas right side up and combines the views from each eye into a three-dimensional image. No wonder picture puzzles can be tough. But puzzles help strengthen your visual perception and cognitive skills, so think of this book as a workout for your brain.

WHAT IN THE WORLD?

Patterns, colors, and shapes help you identify things. The photos in these games show only partial views of animals and objects, which means your brain has to do some heavy lifting to identify what you're seeing. Sound like a challenge that will help bulk up your brain?
HOW TO PLAY: Use photos, written clues, and scrambled words to find the answers.

REAL OR FAKE?

Is seeing always believing? With modern technology, you can never be too sure. On these pages you'll find some truly incredible images of amazing things that really exist in our world—but you'll also find some that are a little too outrageous to be true. You'll have to put on your thinking cap and be super skeptical of these sneaky shots!

HOW TO PLAY: Study the images to decide what is real, and what is really fake!

TAKE A LOOK!

Puzzles like these require you to spend time finding objects, and that helps stretch your attention and memory. While you're searching among a wild jumble of objects for a squirrel or an igloo, you're building brainpower by exercising your concentration skills.
HOW TO PLAY: Find all of the items on the list.

UP CLOSE

Scientists using powerful microscopes can zoom in to reveal stunning details and unseen worlds. The scanning electron microscope (SEM for short) can magnify objects 500,000 times. You may think you're seeing aliens from another planet, so you'll have to flex your logical-thinking muscles to solve these puzzles.

HOW TO PLAY: Match each extreme close-up in the top row with an image in the bottom row.

HIDDEN ANIMALS

Animals often have coloring and patterns that help them blend in with their surroundings and keep them safe from predators. Called camouflage, this trick enables some animals to hide in plain sight! You'll practice attention to detail and visual discrimination strengths with these puzzlers.

HOW TO PLAY: Find the hidden animals in their natural habitats.

OPTICAL ILLUSION

These tricky pics are designed to fool your eyes and brain! Some optical illusions appear to be one thing, but also look like another. This trick works from any viewpoint; it's all about perception: how your brain interprets conflicting information you're seeing.

HOW TO PLAY: Take a second look at the image. Is there another way to interpret these wacky photos?

DOUBLE TAKE

Two seemingly identical photographs filled with multicolored objects present a challenge to find ten differences between the two images. You will use your visual discrimination—the ability to pick out differences and similarities—as well as exercise concentration and short-term memory.

HOW TO PLAY: Find all of the differences between the two photographs.

MORE CHALLENGES

Ready for the next level? This section offers bonus activities that will expand your brain and build your mental fitness, which boosts your ability to think and learn. It's like having a personal trainer for your brain. Fun activities will extend your cognitive brain skills by relating the puzzling pictures in this book to the real world. Create your own cool optical illusions, test your short- and long-term memory, and see how fast your brain can process exciting new challenges.

Everyone's brain works differently, so don't worry if some of the puzzles are difficult at first. They get easier with practice! Answers are on pages 44–46.

SEHROYFL

Whoa, Nelly—this pesky pest packs a big bite! Fortunately it's teeny-tiny compared to its namesake.

KENYOM

Get this one right and you'll be having more fun than a barrel full of ... well ... this animal.

My—what big teeth you have! Better for this massive marine mammal to pull itself up out of the water and onto ice.

SAWLUR

This ssslithering ssspecies has ssspecial heat-detecting sssensors that help it find sssupper.

IPT REVPI

OBX RUTTLE

There's no place like home for this shy reptile—in fact it carries its home right on its back!

OLANIFMG

The pink in the plumage of this feathered flier comes from the shrimp it snacks on.

Listen up! This cuddly cutie is identifiable by its long ears.

IBARTB

You better bring a ladder if you want to see eye to eye with this towering titan.

FRIFAGE

ANIMAL FACES **WHAT IN THE WORLD?**

REAL OR FAKE? EXTREME ADVENTURES

1

2

3

Look! Up in the sky! It's a bird ... It's a plane ... It's a human performing a death-defying stunt? These four images showcase amazing people in incredible situations—but only three of the images are real. Think hot-air-balloon surfing is all the rage? Or that soaring above the water in a jetpack is the latest thing? Or would you rather get a grip on free-climbing cliffs? How about wearing a specialized wingsuit to help you fly through the air? See if you can figure out which of these images are real and which is the fake!

4

Fun Fact!

Flying **squirrels** can **glide** distances up to the length of a **football** field!

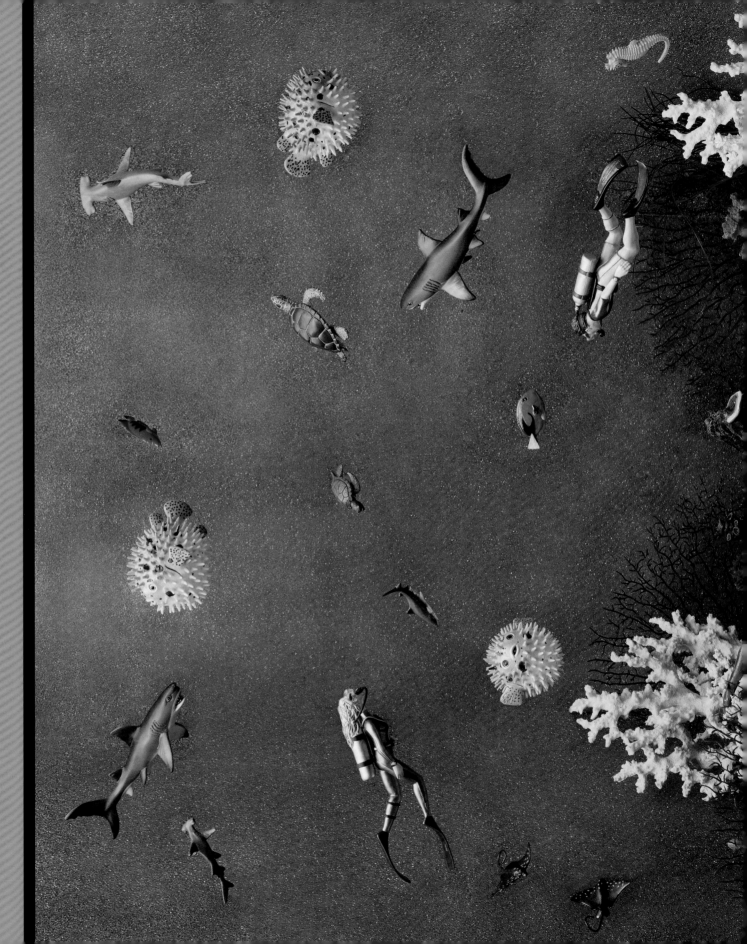

TAKE A LOOK! UNDER THE SEA

< FIND THESE ITEMS IN THE OCEAN. >

3 puffer fish

2 scuba divers

2 octopuses

3 rays

2 crabs

1 ship's wheel

7 sea stars

3 sea turtles

1 sunken treasure chest

8 sharks

1

2

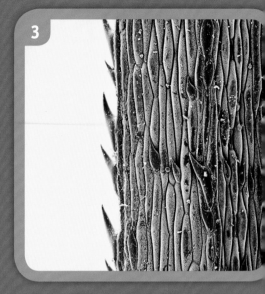
3

FOX FUR

DAISY PETAL

PRICKLY PEAR SPINE

The top row of photographs shows extreme close-ups of the same things that appear in the second row, but in a different order. Match the magnified images with the named objects.

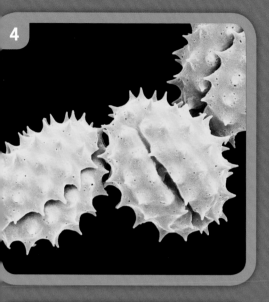

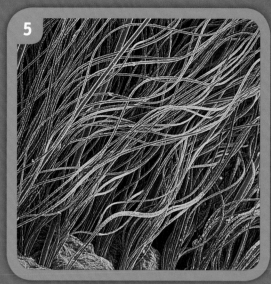

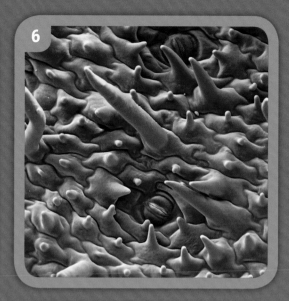

GRASS

HAMMERHEAD SHARKSKIN

POLLEN

EMPEROR SHRIMP

SAND CAT

TREE FROG

CRAB SPIDER

FLOUNDER   WHITE-TAILED PTARMIGANS

HIDDEN ANIMALS CAMOUFLAGE

At first glance you might think this fuzzy little caterpillar is just crawling across a branch. But look again—it's not one animal ... it's nine! These bee-eater birds huddle close together on a brisk day in Spain. Their bright colors create a fluid line, making it tough to tell where one ends and the next one begins!

Fun Fact! **Eggplants** and **tomatoes** both belong to the **same family** as the **deadly nightshade** plant—but **don't worry,** these veggies are **harmless!**

Rain doesn't stop shoppers from buying their fruits and veggies at this outdoor market in Venice, Italy.

When it comes to this frozen feature, there's so much more than meets the eye!

CEERIBG

DASISLN

Deserted or not, these watery wonders have no neighbors.

LAFLAWERT

Stand under this if you're in the mood for rain but there's not a cloud in sight.

LOVCONA

Be careful if you're around one of these when it wakes up, or you'll be feeling hot, hot, hot!

NONCAY

The biggest one in North America sure is *grand!*

STREED

A visit to this dry place will leave you *thirsty* for more!

PROC FESDIL

From high above, these productive places look like a patchwork quilt.

SERFTO

Bears, bunnies, and birds all call this place home.

INTUNSMOA

Scale the highest of these and you'll really be sitting on top of the world!

AMAZING EARTH **WHAT IN THE WORLD?**

Fun Fact!

Moats that surrounded **medieval castles** were often filled with **sharpened sticks** so invaders couldn't **wade across!**

< FIND THESE ITEMS AT THE MEDIEVAL CASTLE. >

10 butterflies

1 cat

4 red birds

4 ladybugs

1 unicorn

3 archers

6 horses

6 knights in shining armor

2 kings

1 beaver

1 wizard

REAL OR FAKE? EXTREME ARCHITECTURE

1

2

3

No need to adjust your book—you're holding it the right way. If these structures seem topsy-turvy, it's because they were built that way! From hobbit houses to twisted towers, upside-down abodes to ice castles, these buildings are totally weird. But do they really exist, or is this awesome architecture just too strange to be true?

Fun Fact!

The largest snowflake ever recorded was bigger than a Frisbee.

1

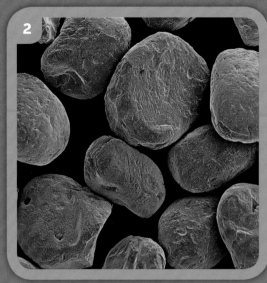

2

3

GUITAR STRINGS

SEAL FUR

SAND

The top row of photographs shows extreme close-ups of the same things that appear in the second row, but in a different order. Match the magnified images with the named objects.

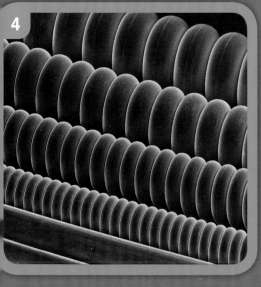

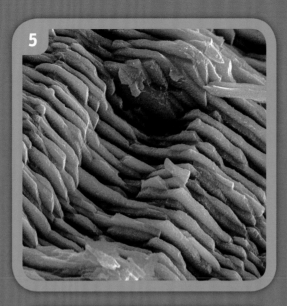

BUTTERFLY

EASTERN BLUEBIRD FEATHER

ABALONE SHELLS

MAGNIFICATION **UP** CLOSE

EUPITHECIA MONTICOLEUS CATERPILLAR

MARKHOR GOAT

ARCTIC FOX

NORTHERN LEAF-TAILED GECKO

JAPANESE MACAQUE **AFRICAN LION**

HIDDEN ANIMALS CAMOUFLAGE

Blink and you'll miss it—this eagle's so fast it leaves a trail of exhaust in its wake! Okay, not really ... but this optical illusion might have you believing otherwise. Captured at the picture-perfect moment, the jets that flew overhead moments before this soaring eagle took flight created an engine-powered trail that gave the fierce flier the look of a superhero.

Fun Fact!

Because of Earth's **tilt**, the Arctic receives 24 hours of sunlight in the summer and 24 hours of **darkness** in the winter.

< FIND THESE ARCTIC ITEMS. >

1 snowman

5 caribou

10 people

10 polar bears

6 orcas (killer whales)

3 walruses

4 harp seals

2 snowy owls

3 arctic hares

6 snowflakes

Fun Fact! The real name of Thailand's capital, **Bangkok,** is the longest place-name on Earth: Krung Thep Mahanakhon Amon Rattanakosin Mahinthara Ayuthaya Mahadilok Phop Noppharat Ratchathani Burirom Udomratchaniwet Mahasathan Amon Piman Awatan Sathit Sakkathattiya Witsanukam Prasit.

People dress up to perform traditional Thai dances at a Rocket Festival in Laos, to celebrate the launch of the harvest season.

You'll stop and take notice when this incredible insect flutters by.

RUFTYBELT

Make a wish on this insect! This member of the beetle family is said to be good luck.

DABGULY

LOW

Whooooo's hiding in this spot? A nocturnal predator with built-in night vision!

This cool kitty has a spotted coat to match its frosty surroundings.

SWNO PREDOLA

LASNADMERA

If the going gets tough, this slippery specimen can ditch its own tail for a quick getaway.

This crafty crustacean is quick to snap a colossal claw when it finds itself in a pinch.

SOBRELT

GRITE YILL

Is it flower or feline? This green grower has a brain-boggling name.

Giddyup for a ride on this fine equine!

SHERO

HELAW KRASH

Don't be fooled by the fearsome name. This biggest fish in the sea is actually as friendly as can be!

SPOTS IN NATURE **WHAT IN THE WORLD?**

REAL OR FAKE? UNBELIEVABLE ANIMALS

1

3

2

Animals with weird patterns, funky fur, and freaky features can be found all over the animal kingdom. We know it's a wonderfully wacky world out there, but are some of these animals just a little *too* wacky? Tune in to your truth-o-meter and see if you can determine which of these animals are real, and which are really fake.

Fun Fact!

Animals with **antlers** shed them **once a year.** Animals with **horns** grow them for **life.**

PUFF ADDER SNAKE

KATYDID

HERCULES MOTH

BANDED WOODPECKER

WHITE-TAILED DEER

CHEETAH

HIDDEN ANIMALS CAMOUFLAGE

Do you always trust your eyes? Well, in that case, you might think someone went camping in the clouds. But look again—where this tent was pitched is actually just snow, but the clouds behind this mountaintop make it appear as though the tent is floating in the air.

TAKE A LOOK!

NATIONAL PARK

< FIND THESE NATIONAL PARK ITEMS. >

1 raccoon

5 wolves

4 bears

1 bald eagle

2 squirrels

2 beavers

7 animals with
antlers

2 bison

2 foxes

MORE CHALLENGES

HUNGRY FOR MORE BRAIN-BOGGLING PUZZLES to further hone your budding brilliance? No problem! You can turn the puzzles you've already completed into new challenges using the tips in this section, or create your own at home to stump your friends and family. There's no reason the fun has to end just because the book does!

WHAT IN THE REAL WORLD?

What in the World? is a game of up-close images that challenge our brains to think in a different direction and use clues to solve puzzles. Try these variations to further mold your mind:

Animal Faces: pages 6–7

- Play your own version of the animal faces game using your own photos. Ask your friends and family to give you pictures of their faces. Lay all of them out on a table and use sticky notes to cover up most of each picture except one feature (mouth or nose, for example). Write clues for each photo and see how many your friends and family can get right!

Amazing Earth: pages 18–19

- Get outside for this challenge! Visit a park or just go out into your own backyard. Collect fallen leaves or flowers. Ask an adult to help you figure out what in the world they are.
- Try to figure out where the leaves or flowers came from. Do you see a tree nearby that matches the leaf that fell on the ground? Or do you think it blew in from a tree farther away?

Spots in Nature: pages 32–33

- This game helps you identify a pattern in nature (in this case, spots). A pattern is something that repeats. See how many patterns you can identify in your own home!
- Can you think of other animals that have spots that are not pictured in the game?

REAL OR FAKE?

They used to say that a picture was worth a thousand words. But with today's advanced technology it's pretty easy to fake a photo of something that never happened or doesn't really exist. And with the easy access to all of the information out there, it's even easier to believe it! Practice refining your detective skills with these tips and tricks:

- Ask questions: Does the photo look a little too unbelievable? Do you think it's possible to accomplish the feat pictured in the image? Where could this picture have been taken? If it seems impossible, it just might be.
- Look for telltale signs of digital alterations. Is the horizon even? Do the borders match up? Is there a mistake the photoshop artist didn't catch?
- Dig for the truth. Enlist the help of a trusted adult to do a quick web search. There are plenty of sources out there doing the research for you that can give you the full answer in an instant.
- Go with your gut. Usually your first instinct is the right one. If something feels off, it probably is.

TAKE ANOTHER LOOK!

There's much more to discover in these puzzles! Here's a list of some ways to test your powers of observation:

Ocean: pages 10–11

- How many different types of coral are in this scene?
- Count the number of red things you see.
- Do you spot a funny sign?
- How many different species of animals are in the photo?
- How many mammals do you see?

Medieval Castle: pages 20–21

- Count how many animals in the scene have four legs.
- Identify all of the insects.
- How many medieval weapons do you see?
- Do you spot the moat?
- Count all of the things that fly.

The Arctic: pages 28–29

- How many trees do you see?
- Identify all of the baby animals.
- How many deadly animals do you see in the photo?

National Park: pages 38–39

- Count the number of birds.
- Do you see the two wolf cubs? What are they doing?
- How many animals in the picture hibernate?
- Count the number of brown animals.
- Can you spot the nocturnal animal?
- Can you spot the animal den?

UP CLOSE—GET EVEN CLOSER!

It's very cool to get up close and personal to things you can see in the world around you ... but do you know what's even cooler? The things you can't see! Everyday objects viewed under a microscope turn out to be much more complex than you'd ever imagine. Here are ten things to check out:

- A leaf
- A piece of fruit
- A hair follicle
- Pet hair
- Sand
- A worm or insect
- Fabric
- A droplet of water
- Your skin
- A snowflake (For this one, catch a snowflake on a piece of black construction paper and immediately put it into the freezer for later viewing!)

MORE CHALLENGES

SPOTTING HIDDEN ANIMALS

Every hour of every day, chances are there's an insect just a few feet away. These tiny creatures are the most abundant animal category in the world—with ants outnumbering humans a million to one! They shouldn't be too hard to spot ... or are they? It's a bug-eat-bug world out there, and these creatures are pretty crafty when it comes to hiding in plain sight. Here are some tips for spotting several species:

- Go outside. While it's true that insects often can be found indoors, it's easiest to see them in their natural habitat.
- Look for places insects like to hide: Search inside flowers, peek under logs, lift up a damp rock, or dig a little in the dirt.
- When you spot an insect, don't touch! Snap a quick photo with your camera.
- Be careful! Anyone who has ever been stung by a bee or wasp can tell you it's no walk in the park, and sometimes people who have allergies to these insects can get very sick very quickly. Check with a parent or guardian before you go on your bug hunt, and if you stray outside your backyard have a trusted adult with you.

SPOTTING OPTICAL ILLUSIONS IN NATURE

Optical illusions are everywhere—it's simply a matter of training your brain to see them. Take clouds, for example. Have you ever looked up in the sky and seen a dog, a dinosaur, or maybe even your little brother? You know that's not really an animal or person—it's an optical illusion. Here are some tips for discovering where and when to check out these sneaky sights:

- When you observe forms in nature, take in the whole sight. Some people looking at the image above might notice only a soaring eagle. But when you take into account the jet exhaust in the background, it looks as if that eagle is flying at turbo speed!
- Shadows and perspective make for great optical illusions. Have you ever been walking with the sun at your back and seen your shadow stretched out in front of you? Sometimes it appears to be the shadow of someone who is eight feet (2.4 m) tall! That's because the position of the sun is low enough that when it hits your back and casts a shadow, it stretches the shadow out along the sidewalk in front of you.
- Have you ever heard of a mirage? One type of mirage occurs in nature when a surface is hotter than the air above it. If you look at a highway stretched out on a hot summer day you might see water pooling on the road ahead of you. That's not water—it's actually an optical illusion!

DOUBLE TAKE TWO

Want to quiz your friends and fool your family with more puzzles like the "Double Take" games in this book? Try these activities in a group or on your own:

- Flex those short-term-memory muscles! Go back to the farmers' market image on pages 16–17. Spend a minute or two looking at one of the photos and trying to memorize the details. Then close the book and write down as many things as you can remember. How many did you get right? What did you miss? Did you write down something that's not in the picture? Repeat the same exercise using the image on pages 30–31.

- For a long-term-memory test, do the same exercise as above, but look at the photos in the morning and then wait until evening—or the next day—to write the list. Do it again a week later and see if your memory improved!

- Turn your bedroom into a double take. Take a picture of how it normally looks. Then rearrange ten things and take the picture again. Print both pictures and lay them side by side. See if your friends or family can spot the differences!

- Practice doing picture puzzles with a timer to increase your brain's processing speed.

TITLE PAGE
(pages 2–3)

A female saturniid moth uses her flashy colors to blend in perfectly with leaves on the forest floor in China's Qinling Mountains.

WHAT IN THE WORLD?
(pages 6–7)

Top row: parrot fish, walrus, horsefly, pit viper, monkey. **Bottom row:** rabbit, box turtle, giraffe, flamingo.

REAL OR FAKE?
(pages 8–9)

1. fake, 2. real, 3. real, 4. real

TAKE A LOOK!
(pages 10–11)

UP CLOSE
(pages 12–13)

1. prickly pear spine, 2. hammerhead sharkskin, 3. daisy petal, 4. pollen, 5. fox fur, 6. grass

HIDDEN ANIMALS
(page 14)

OPTICAL ILLUSION
(page 15)

Illusion explained: Zoom in on this creepy-crawly, and you'll realize you're not staring at a fuzzy insect, but a group of fluffy birds! It's hard to pick them out individually, which demonstrates an important concept in animal behavior—safety in numbers! This behavior is often seen among zebras, which stick together in a herd. Observing the confusing stripes of a group of zebras, a predator has a hard time singling out one zebra. Animals also stick together for another important reason: warmth. This optical illusion is actually survival 101!

DOUBLE TAKE
(pages 16–17)

WHAT IN THE WORLD?
(pages 18–19)

Top row: iceberg, islands, waterfall, volcano, canyon. **Bottom row:** desert, crop fields, forest, mountains.

TAKE A LOOK!
(pages 20–21)

REAL OR FAKE?
(pages 22–23)

1. real, 2. real, 3. real, 4. fake

UP CLOSE
(pages 24–25)

1. butterfly, 2. sand, 3. eastern bluebird feather, 4. guitar strings, 5. abalone shells, 6. seal fur

HIDDEN ANIMALS
(page 26)

OPTICAL ILLUSION
(page 27)

Illusion explained: Talk about perfect timing! Two images in the sky combine at exactly the right moment to create this picture-perfect optical illusion. A passing jet that had already disappeared from the camera frame left a trail of exhaust painted across the sky. An eagle passed by the right place at the right time, and voilà! You almost can't believe your eyes!

TAKE A LOOK!
(pages 28–29)

DOUBLE TAKE
(pages 30–31)

WHAT IN THE WORLD?
(pages 32–33)

Top row: butterfly, ladybug, owl, snow leopard, salamander. **Bottom row:** lobster, tiger lily, horse, whale shark.

SHHH! ANSWERS

REAL OR FAKE?
(pages 34–35)

1. real, 2. real, 3. real, 4. fake

HIDDEN ANIMALS
(page 36)

OPTICAL ILLUSION
(page 37)

Illusion explained: Do you always trust your eyes? Well, in that case, you might think someone went camping in the clouds. But look again—where this tent was pitched is actually just snow, but the clouds behind this mountaintop make it appear as though the tent is floating in the air.

TAKE A LOOK!
(pages 38–39)

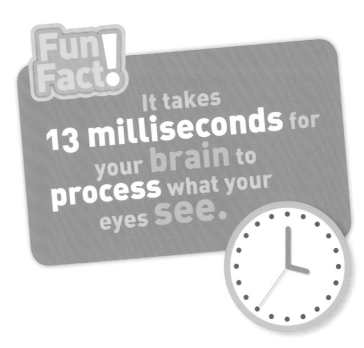

Fun Fact!

It takes **13 milliseconds** for your **brain** to **process** what your eyes **see**.

MORE TO EXPLORE

HAVE FUN EXPLORING more optical illusions, puzzles, and games with these websites, books, and other resources.

WEBSITES

kids.nationalgeographic.com
This site inspires curious kids and makes learning fun. Check out the games section!

kids.niehs.nih.gov/index.htm
Discover tons of games at this "Kids' Pages" site from the National Institute of Environmental Health Sciences.

kidskonnect.com
A safe Internet gateway that is loaded with brain games just for kids.

lumosity.com
A website where people of all ages can build a personalized brain-training program.

BOOKS & MAGAZINES

Xtreme Illusions and Xtreme Illusions 2
National Geographic Society, 2012 and 2014
Mind-bending collections of visual puzzles that will amaze your friends, mystify your family, and blow your own mind!

The Big Book of Fun!
National Geographic Society, 2010
Check out these boredom-busting games, jokes, puzzles, mazes, and more!

Complete Guide to Brain Health
By Michael S. Sweeney
National Geographic Society, 2013
A book for the whole family to learn simple exercises that can strengthen your brain.

Brain Games
By Jennifer Swanson
National Geographic Society, 2015
Time to exercise your noggin and have a blast doing it. A superfun compilation of challenges, myths, fun facts, science, and games all about your brain!

Brain Works
By Michael S. Sweeney
National Geographic Society, 2011
This book for adults and kids reveals the mind-bending science of how you see, what you think, and who you are. Includes cool optical illusions.

Mastermind
By Stephanie Drimmer
National Geographic Society, 2015
Test your smarts with interactive puzzles and games, and learn how to unleash your inner genius.

National Geographic Kids magazine
Dare to explore! Look for visual games and activities in the "Fun Stuff" department.

TELEVISION

Grab a parent and tune in to **Brain Games** on the National Geographic Channel.
Parents: **braingames.nationalgeographic.com**

CREDITS

STAFF FOR THIS BOOK

Kate Olesin, *Project Editor*
Callie Broaddus, *Art Director*
Lisa Jewell, *Photo Editor*
Paige Towler, *Editorial Assistant*
Rachel Kenny and Sanjida Rashid, *Design Production Assistants*
Michael Cassady, *Rights Clearance Specialist*
Grace Hill, *Managing Editor*
Joan Gossett, *Senior Production Editor*
Lewis R. Bassford, *Production Manager*
Rachel Faulise, *Manager, Production Services*
Susan Borke, *Legal and Business Affairs*

PUBLISHED BY THE NATIONAL GEOGRAPHIC SOCIETY

Gary E. Knell, *President and CEO*
John M. Fahey, *Chairman of the Board*
Melina Gerosa Bellows, *Chief Education Officer*
Declan Moore, *Chief Media Officer*
Hector Sierra, *Senior Vice President and General Manager, Book Division*

SENIOR MANAGEMENT TEAM, KIDS PUBLISHING AND MEDIA

Nancy Laties Feresten, *Senior Vice President;* Jennifer Emmett, *Vice President, Editorial Director, Kids Books;* Julie Vosburgh Agnone, *Vice President, Editorial Operations;* Rachel Buchholz, *Editor and Vice President, NG Kids magazine;* Michelle Sullivan, *Vice President, Kids Digital;* Eva Absher-Schantz, *Design Director;* Jay Sumner, *Photo Director;* Hannah August, *Marketing Director;* R. Gary Colbert, *Production Director*

DIGITAL

Anne McCormack, *Director;* Laura Goertzel, Sara Zeglin, *Producers;* Emma Rigney, *Creative Producer;* Bianca Bowman, *Assistant Producer;* Natalie Jones, *Senior Product Manager*

The National Geographic Society is one of the world's largest nonprofit scientific and educational organizations. Founded in 1888 to "increase and diffuse geographic knowledge," the Society's mission is to inspire people to care about the planet. It reaches more than 400 million people worldwide each month through its official journal, *National Geographic*, and other magazines; National Geographic Channel; television documentaries; music; radio; films; books; DVDs; maps; exhibitions; live events; school publishing programs; interactive media; and merchandise. National Geographic has funded more than 10,000 scientific research, conservation, and exploration projects and supports an education program promoting geographic literacy.

FOR MORE INFORMATION, please visit www.nationalgeographic.com, call 1-800-NGS LINE (647-5463), or write to the following address:

National Geographic Society
1145 17th Street N.W.
Washington, D.C. 20036-4688 U.S.A.

Visit us online at nationalgeographic.com/books

For librarians and teachers: ngchildrensbooks.org

More for kids from National Geographic:
kids.nationalgeographic.com

For information about special discounts for bulk purchases, please contact National Geographic Books Special Sales: ngspecsales@ngs.org

For rights or permissions inquiries, please contact National Geographic Books Subsidiary Rights: ngbookrights@ngs.org

Hardcover ISBN: 978-1-4263-2080-4
Reinforced library binding ISBN: 978-1-4263-2081-1

Printed in China
15/RRDS/1

ILLUSTRATIONS

COVER: Inset (UP RT), Nazzu/Shutterstock; (Background), BreatheFitness/iStock; (LO LE), TheRocky41/Shutterstock; (RT), FGorgun/iStock; (UP LE), Jasmina007/iStock; BACK COVER, Alfredo Estrella/AFP/Getty Images; SPINE, Nazzu/Shutterstock; 1 (UP LE), Taiga/Dreamstime; 1 (CTR RT), Songquan Deng/Dreamstime; 1 (UP CTR), Bill Heinsohn/Getty Images; 1 (LO CTR), Ted Kinsman/Science Source; 1 (CTR), OceanwideImages.com; 1 (LO LE), SuperStock/Alamy; 1 (CTR LE), Ferrero-Labat/Minden Pictures; 1 (UP RT), Ted Kinsman/Science Source; 1 (LO RT), Alex Hyde/Nature Picture Library; 2-3, Thomas Marent/Minden Pictures; 4 (LE), Jonathan R. Green/Dreamstime; 4 (UP RT), Jaime Jacott/REX USA; 4 (LO RT), Rebecca Hale/NGS Staff; 5 (UP RT), Tupungato/Shutterstock; 5 (LO), Jose Luis Rodriguez; 5 (UP), Ted Kinsman/Science Source; 5 (CTR LE), John Cancalosi/ARDEA; 6, Franco Banfi/Nature Picture Library; 7 (LO LE), Marc Parsons/Shutterstock; 7 (LO CTR LE), djem/Shutterstock; 7 (LO RT), Oleksii Sergieiev/Dreamstime; 7 (LO CTR RT), Icelaw/Dreamstime; 7 (UP CTR), Callmedik/Dreamstime; 7 (UP LE), Fuse/Getty Images; 7 (UP CTR LE), Entomologist and Nature Photographer, Portugal/Getty Images; 7 (UP RT), Berendje Photography/Shutterstock; 8 (CTR LE), topseller/Shutterstock; 8 (LO RT), Photobac/Shutterstock; 8 (UP CTR), Darren Baker/Shutterstock; 8 (UP RT), Ruth Peterkin/Shutterstock; 9, Oliver Furrer Image Source/Newscom; 10-11, Rebecca Hale/NGS Staff; 11 (UP RT), Tolly81/Dreamstime; 12 (LO CTR), Curtis Hofer/Dreamstime; 12 (LO LE), Jaymudaliar/Dreamstime; 12 (LO RT), Gabriel Walter Farmer 1/Shutterstock; 12 (UP CTR), Ted Kinsman/Science Source; 12 (UP LE), Biophoto Associates/Science Source; 12 (UP RT), Biophoto Associates/Science Source; 13 (LO CTR), Martin Strmiska/Alamy; 13 (LO LE), Paul Richards/Dreamstime; 13 (LO RT), Grigoriy Pil/Dreamstime; 13 (UP CTR), Susumu Nishinaga/Science Source; 13 (UP LE), Mediscan/Alamy; 13 (UP RT), Eye of Science/Science Source; 14 (LO LE), Visuals Unlimited/Corbis; 14 (LO RT), Donald M. Jones/Minden Pictures; 14 (UP CTR), Thomas Rabeil/Nature Picture Library; 14 (UP LE), blickwinkel/Alamy; 14 (UP RT), Jurgen Freund/Nature Picture Library; 14 (UP CTR RT), Alex Hyde/Nature Picture Library; 15, Jose Luis Rodriguez; 16, Tupungato/Shutterstock; 16 (LO), Evgenyi44/Dreamstime; 17, Tupungato/Shutterstock; 18, Jonathan R. Green/Dreamstime; 19 (LO LE), Taiga/Dreamstime; 19 (LO LE), imageBROKER/SuperStock; 19 (LO RT), Ingridneumann/Dreamstime; 19 (LO CTR RT), imageBROKER/SuperStock; 19 (UP LE), Vicki Beaver/Alamy; 19 (UP CTR LE), Songquan Deng/Dreamstime; 19 (UP RT), Bill Heinsohn/Getty Images; 19 (UP RT), Travel Library Limited/Travel Library Limited/SuperStock; 20-21, Rebecca Hale/NGS Staff; 20 (LE), Filip Lenkiewicz/Dreamstime; 21 (UP RT), Walter Quirtmair/Shutterstock; 22 (LO LE), Saskia Schutter/ZUMAPRESS/Newscom; 22 (RT), View Pictures/Rex/REX USA; 22 (UP LE), Jaime Jacott/REX USA; 23, George Hammerstein/Corbis; 24 (LO CTR), Arco Images GmbH/Alamy; 24 (LO LE), Mike Ehrman/Dreamstime; 24 (LO RT), Jim Parkin/Dreamstime; 24 (UP CTR), David Scharf/Science Source; 24 (UP LE), Deco Images II/Alamy; 24 (UP RT), Ted Kinsman/Science Source; 25 (LO CTR), Steve Byland/Dreamstime; 25 (LO LE), Tim Fitzharris/Minden Pictures; 25 (LO RT), Kaye Eileen Oberstar/Dreamstime; 25 (UP CTR), Ted Kinsman/Science Source; 25 (UP LE), David Scharf/Science Source; 25 (UP RT), Steve Gschmeissner/Science Source; 26 (CTR), Matthias Breiter/Minden Pictures; 26 (LO LE), Cyril Ruoso/Minden Pictures; 26 (LO RT), Gerry Ellis/Getty Images; 26 (UP CTR), Darlyne A. Murawski/Getty Images; 26 (UP LE), Eric Dragesco/Nature Picture Library; 26 (UP RT), Martin Mullis/Minden Pictures; 27, Pam Mullins/Caters News Agency; 28-29, Rebecca Hale/NGS Staff; 28 (LE), Vismax/Dreamstime; 29 (UP), NASA/Handout/Getty Images; 30, Visun Khankasem/Shutterstock; 31, Visun Khankasem/Shutterstock; 32, Rolf Nussbaumer Photography/Alamy; 33 (LO LE), OceanwideImages.com; 33 (LO CTR LE), SuperStock/Alamy; 33 (LO RT), Martin Strmiska/Alamy; 33 (LO CTR RT), Adam Goss/Dreamstime; 33 (UP LE), Morskaya20031/Dreamstime; 33 (UP CTR LE), Nico Smit/Dreamstime; 33 (UP RT), Miroslav Hlavko/Dreamstime; 33 (UP CTR RT), Arco Images GmbH/Alamy; 34 (LO LE), Jan-Philipp Strobel/dpa/Corbis; 34 (RT), AP Photo/A. Fifis Ifremer; 34 (UP LE), Chris Lukhaup; 35, Chase Swift/Corbis; 36 (LO LE), W. Perry Conway/Corbis; 36 (LO RT), Ferrero-Labat/Minden Pictures; 36 (UP CTR), Solvin Zankl/Nature Picture Library; 36 (CTR), Gerry Ellis/Minden Pictures; 36 (UP LE), John Cancalosi/ARDEA; 36 (UP RT), Neil Bowman/Minden Pictures; 37, Bjarke Bitsch/Solent News/Rex/REX USA; 38-39, Rebecca Hale/NGS Staff; 38 (LE), Eric Honeycutt/Dreamstime; 40 (UP), Chase Swift/Corbis; 40 (LO), Bill Heinsohn/Getty Images; 41 (UP LE), Rebecca Hale/NGS Staff; 41 (LO RT), Ted Kinsman/Science Source; 42 (LO), John Cancalosi/ARDEA; 42 (UP), Pam Mullins/Caters News Agency; 43, Tupungato/Shutterstock; 46 (LO LE), Vicki Beaver/Alamy; 47, SuperStock/Alamy